GOLF INSTRUCTOR'S LIBRARY

ON THE GREEN

MICHAEL HOBBS

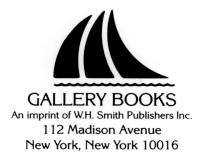

GALLERY BOOKS

An imprint of W.H. Smith Publishers Inc.
112 Madison Avenue
New York, New York 10016

A QUINTET BOOK

Produced for GALLERY BOOKS
An imprint of W. H. Smith Publishers Inc.
112 Madison Avenue
New York, New York 10016

ISBN 0–8317–3874–X

This book was designed and produced by
Quintet Publishing Limited
6 Blundell Street
London N7 9BH

Creative Director: Terry Jeavons
Art Director: Ian Hunt
Project Editor: David Barraclough
Illustrator: Rob Shone
Photographer: Michael Hobbs

Typeset in Great Britain by
Central Southern Typesetters, Eastbourne
Manufactured in Hong Kong by
Regent Publishing Services Limited
Printed in Hong Kong by
Leefung-Asco Printers Limited

**Although the PGA now officially uses the term 'the
hold', throughout this book refers to 'the grip', which is
still commonly used among golfers.**

CONTENTS

PREFACE

I am a left-handed golfer. However, over the years I haven't found it difficult to follow golf instruction writing, which is traditionally directed at right-handers.

As a golf writer, I know that always mentioning each form of the golfing species is easily possible, but leads to many repetitive phrases that impair the readability of the book. As a left-hander I know we have learned to cope in a 90 per cent right-handed world. A right-hander, on the other hand, is far less able. I don't think he could follow a text written for left-handers – imagine him trying to use left-handed scissors or knock in a tack, grasping the hammer left-handed. What injuries and incompetence would result for this less adaptable and accomplished sector of the human species!

ACKNOWLEDGEMENTS

Above all, I should like to thank Grenville Warne for being a splendid model for my instructional photography. He gave up many hours throughout a whole season when he would surely far rather have been playing than demonstrating. His help has been invaluable.

I should like to thank my main golf club, Tracy Park near Bristol, England, for allowing me to carry out most of the instruction photography on its splendid 27 holes. I also thank other clubs for more limited photographic facilities.

The club's professional, Grant Aitken, and his son and assistant professional Kelvin, have also been invariably helpful with advice, information and allowing me to use equipment for illustrations.

At Quintet Publishing, I should particularly like to thank David Barraclough for his continuous work throughout the project and also Peter Arnold who was responsible for the detailed copy editing. My thanks are also due to Rob Shone for his production of drawings and diagrams and the design team at Bridgewater Design.

Michael Hobbs   Worcester, England

CHAPTER ONE

GRIPS

I t's an old saying that more matches are won and lost on the green than anywhere else. A player who can get down in two putts rather than three will probably beat an opponent who can drive 50 yards farther. It follows, therefore, that anything you can do to eliminate that extra putt will pay huge dividends in terms of winning matches. And it all starts with the grip.

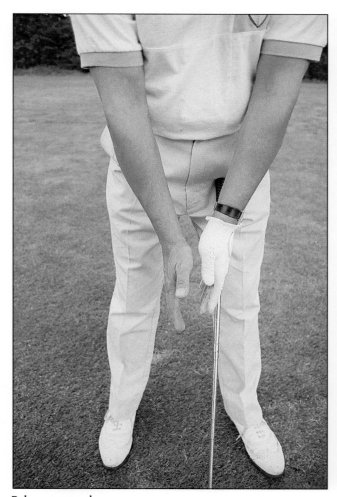

Palms opposed.

Adding the putter.

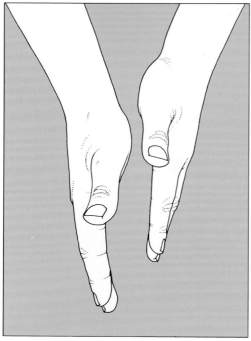

Palms opposed.

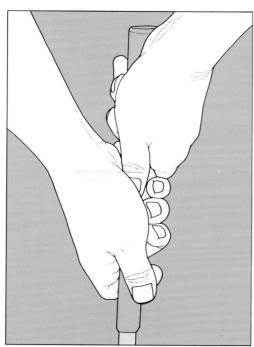

All fingers on the grip.

There is a tremendous variety of ways of holding the club when putting – you can get away with far more unorthodoxy than you ever can when playing full shots.

Nevertheless, you have to know the rules before you can break them with impunity, and there are certain basics which you ignore at your peril. For example, the vast majority of grips for putting are based on presenting the back of the left hand and the palm of the right hand to the hole; in other words, the palms are facing each other.

This gives you a very simple grip check. Simply place the palms together, with the club handle between them, and make sure that both are lined up squarely with the face of your putter.

You'll notice that this gives you one important variation on the way you grip the club for full shots: the top (left) hand will have moved anti-clockwise, while the right hasn't changed.

Having said that, many very good players don't change their grip at all, just because they have reached the green.

Using the same grip on the greens as for long shots.

8

The reverse overlap in close up.

Reverse overlap grip – left forefinger

It can be argued that an unchanged grip feels more natural, and therefore more comfortable. I don't suppose that many golfers instinctively switch to different grips when putting. That probably comes when a player notices what other people are doing, and is spurred into starting to think about it all.

However, why change a winning system? If you find that a normal interlocking or overlapping grip works for you, then I certainly wouldn't be the one to tell you to alter it.

Even so, let's assume that the 'palms-opposed' grip works best for most people and proceed from there. It's sensible to start with the standard grip, and go into a few variations later on.

Because many golfers like to feel that the right hand provides the strike while the left is there principally to support the club, they tend to make sure that all fingers are gripping the club. This, of course, means that the right hand slips down the club a little, and the right little finger no longer overlaps the left forefinger.

Instead, the left hand does some overlapping of its own. It has also slipped a little way down the club, and the left forefinger has come to rest over the bottom hand.

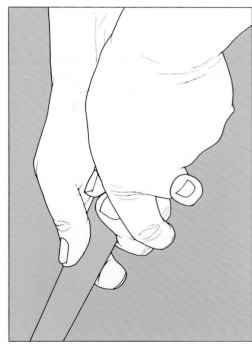

Reverse overlap grip.

9

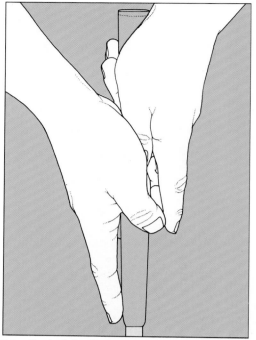

Extending both forefingers.

Both forefingers extended.

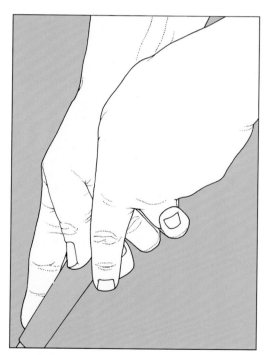

Extending both forefingers – side on.

Just where it comes to rest is largely a matter of personal preference. It can find itself over the little finger of the bottom hand, or at the other extreme, travel downwards until it overlaps the fingertips of the bottom hand. Most people will find that a happy medium works best: somewhere over the knuckles of the right hand.

This is called the 'reverse overlap grip' because it reverses the overlap used for full shots. As always, the object is to encourage the hands to work as one unit.

Extending that forefinger downwards is also helpful in another way. Very slightly, it tightens the sinews of the left wrist, giving a firmer feel to the putting stroke. You'll appreciate just how important this is a little later on.

REVERSE OVERLAP – VARIATIONS

There are a round half-dozen variations of the standard reverse overlap grip. Let's take a look at them.

(1) Don't extend the left forefinger. Just let it come to rest on the putter grip. But don't forget – you do lose that slight tightening of the left wrist.

ABOVE LEFT: Split hands putting.

ABOVE RIGHT: An extreme of the split-hands method.

(2)   The right finger, quite naturally, falls into much the same position for putting as for any other shot. Some good players, however, like to curl it around the handle, while others position it far more loosely, with only the inside of the knuckle in contact. Most people will find the second of these alternatives more successful, because it helps to relax the arm muscles. There is, however, another alternative . . .

(3)   Extend the right forefinger more or less vertically down the handle. This means that both forefingers are now pointing downwards, helping to take the wrists out of the putting stroke, and providing a much more 'arms-only' movement.

This is perhaps the greatest single difference between the basic method used by modern players, when compared with great putters of the past. Walter Hagen and Bobby Jones, for example, were far more wristy than their present-day counterparts.

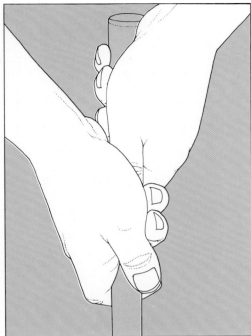

Vardon grip.

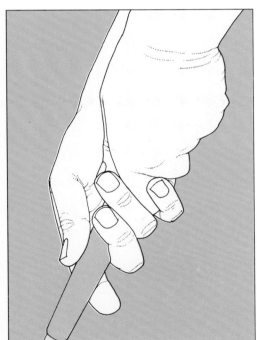

Vardon grip – side on.

LEFT: A green close to water will tend to be damper and putt more slowly.

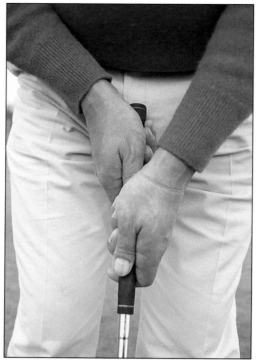

Putting with reversed hands.

It worked superbly for them, but lesser mortals are far better off when this particular source of movement is eliminated from their putting action. Ben Crenshaw provides the clearest example of the arms-only modern method.

Some players like to make that right forefinger the focus of their putting stroke. They like to 'feel' it tapping the ball, and continuing along the target line into the hole.

(4)   Just *where* you place your grip on the club handle is very important indeed, because it affects the feel of the club enormously. At one extreme, that great putter Ray Floyd holds the club at the top of the handle and stands tall as well. Not only that, but he also uses a longer-than-standard shaft.

Other great players like to get nearer to the ball. For example, at the turn of the century, the two greatest names in the game were Harry Vardon and J H Taylor. It has to be said that Vardon wasn't really a better-than-average putter, but, obviously, each of them had legions of imitators. Because both crouched low over the ball when putting, everyone was doing it in no time at all – and the fashion didn't really change until the 1920s.

Bobby Jones, undoubtedly the greatest golfer in the world, came along and putted magnificently, standing comfortably upright. The world duly took note.

Still – if you feel like crouching, you have an excellent alibi for so doing. Andy North does, hands absurdly far down the club, and he's won the US Open twice!)

(5)   Almost as extreme is the practice of leaving the left hand where it is, and setting the bottom hand low down on

Putters come in different shapes. When buying one, make sure you feel comfortable with it; the type of putter head does not matter.

The left wrist has broken.

The Langer grip, not generally recommended, but this really
ensures the left wrist doesn't break.

the handle, leaving a gap between the hands. This invariably
means that the ball strike comes exclusively from the right
hand, and that the left is simply there to steady the club.
Personally, I don't think this method will help the vast
majority of golfers.

Even so, there is a notable devotee of the method in
Hubert Green.

Ray Floyd may well use a longer-than-standard putter,
but some go a great deal further in using a gigantic club with
one grip at the top of the shaft and another halfway down,
leaving a gap of about a couple of feet between the hands.

If you are a thoroughly bad putter, it could be worth
trying one of these monsters, which are a common sight on
the US Senior Tour.

Golfers who have passed their 50th birthday often find
such a club a partial cure for the putting yips, but don't think
that this agonising problem is the exclusive prerogative of the
older player. Sandy Lyle used one for a while early in the 1990
American season, while Sam Torrance, who many had
dismissed as on his way out on the European Tour, found
that the club was a good enough yip cure to enable him to
make the 1989 Ryder Cup team.

(6)   To go to the ultimate extreme, there is no law of
golf which says you have to have both hands on the club at
all, and nothing to say which of the two hands you may use.

I can remember one tournament golfer who used his right hand alone, and employed a very short putter. But – a word of warning – while his method was certainly interesting, it never enabled him to make putting a strong feature of his game. Admittedly, there have been tournament winners who putted with the right hand only. But not for long: it only takes a few mis-hits to destroy confidence in the method, probably forever.

REVERSED HANDS

Some 30 years ago, a South African golfer named Sewsunker Sewgolum caused amazement by winning European tournaments. The raised eyebrows were prompted by the fact that, although right-handed, and standing to the ball that way, he placed his left hand below the right for all shots.

Many children grip the club that way quite naturally, and parents and club professionals are very quick to tell them that you just can't play golf that way. Apart from anything else, the grip isn't much help to most people when it comes to a full swing.

Obviously, no one had told Sewgolum that, and he did go around winning tournaments.

Nevertheless, although this reverse grip isn't suitable for most aspects of play, it can be used successfully on the green. Peter Alliss, Tom Kite, Tony Jacklin and Bernhard Langer, for example, have used the reversed hands method profitably for long periods.

In most cases, the grip is used when the player concerned has developed a nervous tremor in the putting stroke. The method brings into play a whole new set of small muscles, and seems to help eliminate, or at least, ameliorate, the problem.

So it's something to try if you're suffering from mental turmoil on the greens. There are, however, other advantages. In brief, it's worth the experiment if nothing else seems to work.

This is mainly because the commonest fault in putting is the breaking of the left wrist, just before the ball is struck, leading to very inconsistent putting. The left-below-right grip minimizes the likelihood of this happening, because it feels natural to pull the club through with the left hand and arm.

If you think 'pull' to yourself, you won't flick the left hand and wrist at the ball, and if the left wrist is firm, then that's one variable you have eliminated from your game.

Greenside bunkers make approach shots difficult, but the flagstick is well positioned on this green and, once on the putting surface, a standard 'two putt' should be no problem.

CHOOSING A PUTTER

Before sitting down to write this chapter, I conducted a very small piece of research. I visited my pro's shop and counted just how many different types of putter they could offer me. The total was a staggering 113 clubs in 47 different models, the differences between them ranging from the fundamental to the insignificant.

So what does Mr or Ms Beginner do when faced with such a bewildering array of choices? Probably pick out one or two and waft them about in the air, I should think, and then probably try them out on a strip of carpet to see which works best.

Because of the large choice of putters available, your local professional will be only too pleased to let you try them out before making your purchase.

A putter, plus a wood and either the four even
or five odd numbers make up a half-set
of irons.

Which is all very well, but not nearly enough like the real
world to serve any useful purpose.

To start with, no strip of carpet is anything like a green,
be it ever so well manicured. Furthermore, the distance
between the edge of the green and the hole is very much
longer than the pro's floor covering. To see how a putter
performs, you really must try it away from the cosy haven of
the shop, on the green itself.

This is where supporting your club pro, rather than a
sports shop or a department store, really pays off. After all,
the average shopkeeper won't be very keen on watching you
disappear over the horizon with an armful of sample putters.
In contrast, your pro will almost certainly encourage you to
try out a club or two on the practice green, possibly taping
the clubhead to prevent scratches.

Alternatively, you could avoid worrying him by
experimenting with the selection of used clubs which will
invariably be in stock. In addition, you could take any
opportunity to try putters belonging to your fellow golfers.

All this is infinitely preferable to yielding to impulse
and buying putter after putter in the hope that the law of
averages will, sooner or later, produce your own, individual,
magic wand.

The only way to get a feel for certain features of these
clubs is to experiment at every possible opportunity. For
example, if you eventually come to prefer standing fairly

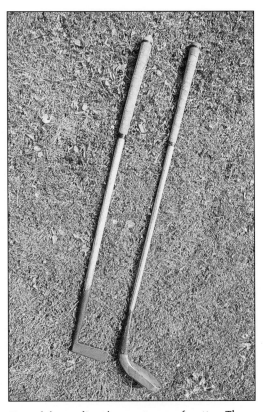

Two of the earliest known types of putter. The
one on the left is very heavy and the wooden
one is far longer in the shaft than would find
favour with today's golfers.

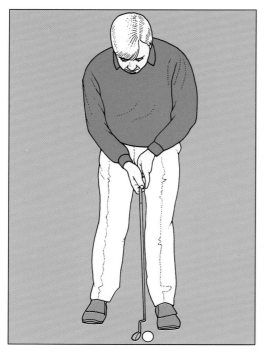

Reverse overlap grip.

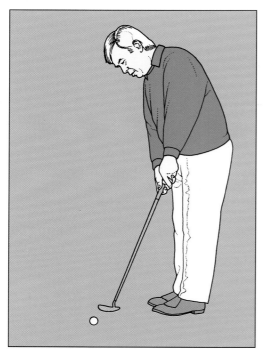

Double overlapping grip.

This putter is similar to those used at the turn of the century by such great players as Harry Vardon, James Braid and John B. Taylor.

upright to the ball, you'll probably need a putter with a shaft of above-average length, and if it's not upright in lie, you'll find yourself stubbing the toe. Conversely, the reverse applies if you crouch over the ball, or prefer standing with your hands close to your body.

Weight is another vital consideration. Some players come to prefer a heavy head, enabling you always to strike the ball gently, unless you're faced with a long putt. Others hold the reverse opinion, finding that heavy clubs seem likely to send the ball streaking past the hole, and that they can never bring themselves to swing the club at all freely.

Which are you? Only experiment will tell. Just as important, you will want to avoid buying a club which doesn't really suit your style, and which leads to adjusting your method to suit the club you've chosen.

All these things seem very obvious when they're written down, but many, many golfers go through their entire golfing lives without such basic principles even occurring to them. The words to remember are 'lie, length and weight'. They apply whichever make or model of club you try, ranging from the most traditional to the strangest of new patents.

What about the flex of the shaft? There isn't really any need to get too complicated about this: extreme flex combined with a heavy head is to be avoided, and so is a rigid shaft and a light head, which can make you feel you're playing with a stick in your hands. I suspect, however, that the average golfer is unaware of the characteristics of his or her putter shaft, and perhaps that's as it should be. What you don't know about, won't worry you.

An undulating two-tier green well protected by a ditch.

PUTTER TYPES

In common with all other conventional golf clubs, the first putters were made of wood, although iron putters soon arrived on the scene. Wood reigned supreme throughout the 19th century, however, and putters looked very much like the drivers and fairway woods of the time. Greens were rough, by modern standards, and putters had whippy shafts and needed quite a long sweeping swing to be effective. About three inches shorter than today, putters were very much flatter in lie, so the player needed to stand well away from the ball. Before pitching clubs were introduced, putters were often used from many yards short of the green.

A modern day metal-headed putter. The head is heavier than most putters but many golfers prefer a putter with weight in the clubhead.

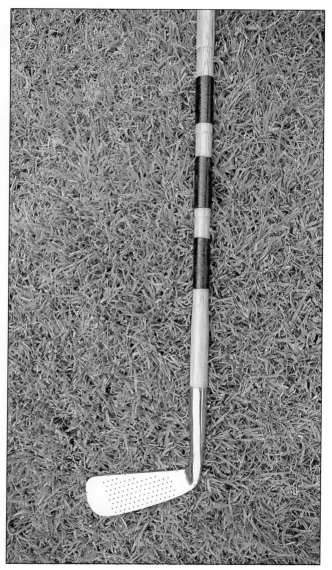

A modern reproduction of the putter used by Bobby Jones.

BELOW AND LEFT: The Schenectady Putter was the first centre shafter putter to be seen in Britain when Walter Travis used it on his way to winning the 1904 British Amateur Championship. The legality of the putter was challenged and it was outlawed in Britain until 1949 when the ban was lifted.

As the century wound on, and irons became increasingly popular, it was natural that metal should be used for putters as well. The wooden club gradually faded out, but when white metal heads became all the rage, some models retained the traditional shape of the head of the wooden model. This kind of head still survives, notably in the shape of the Ray Cook and other models. In putting, as in most other items of golf equipment, there is seldom anything entirely new under the sun.

Iron clubs eventually took over, and except for the length of the shaft and loft, they didn't look so very different from a 1-iron. Both, until the 1930s, had hickory shafts and putters were usually much lighter, and considerably more lofted, than those in use today. This type still survives, usually with a flange along the back to provide more weight.

It may surprise you to learn that the centre shaft was first used early this century; the American, Walter Travis used one when winning the British Amateur Championship in 1904. It was called the 'Schenectady', and was regarded as a magic club. Perhaps the Royal and Ancient thought it unfair for they banned it a few years later. The ban lasted about 40 years, although centre shafts continued to be used in countries which adhered to the rules of golf as decreed by the United States Golf Association.

Today, most putters have the shaft attached at some point between the heel and the centre of the club, rather than at the heel itself, the basic idea being that putting is easier if you are striking the ball fairly close to the end of the shaft. This is certainly something well worth thinking about.

In the 1960s the American, Karsten Solheim, invented what is arguably the most revolutionary putter of all. He realised that many putts which finish short of the hole aren't a matter of misjudgement of length, so much as failure to strike the ball with the right part of the club, and on many traditional putters, that 'sweet spot' is very small indeed.

He solved this problem by placing most of the weight towards the heel and toe, providing a worthwhile margin for error in the middle where one hadn't existed before.

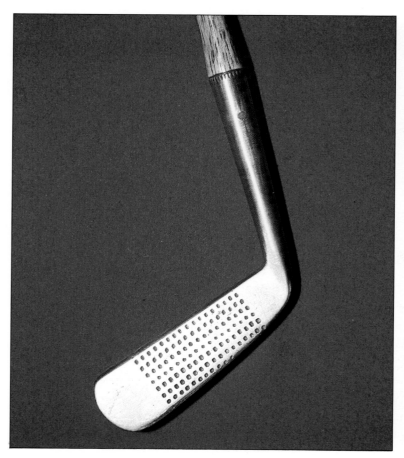

ABOVE: A 1920s putter.

Most golf clubs have practice greens which are manicured the same as the putting surface on the course. You are advised to spend ten minutes or so on the practice green before starting your round. That way you will get the 'feel' of the greens.

Of course, in Solheim's 'Ping' clubs, there is still an optimum spot with which to strike the ball, but if you fail to find it, a slight mis-hit gets you closer to the hole than you would have been with a blade putter.

When you watch tournament players, take note of the surprising number of them who use either 'Ping' putters, or some other heel-and-toe weighted designs.

If you want to make a living from the game, then good putting is an essential, and you'll be aware that many events are won by the player whose game is in good order, and who also turns out to be the best putter of the week.

There are very few professionals who haven't tried out hundreds of putters, so they have much more information on the subject than most of us. What they eventually use is therefore much more significant than the more casual choices of club golfers.

'Trying out' is one thing, but building up a stock of them is expensive, and I don't advise it. Think of Bernhard Langer, for example, renowned for his gallant, though temporary, conquests of his extreme problems on the green. He didn't really become a force to be reckoned with until he found a

BELOW: Lead tape has also been added to this putter, but the cutaway behind the face makes an ideal place for adding 'extra weight'.

ABOVE: To gain extra weight to the clubhead the reverse of the face has leaded tape added to it.

LEFT: The Goose Neck (or Wry-Neck) putter is one of the most popular types of putter. The line of the shaft, when looking down it from the putting position, is slightly in advance of the putter head. This picture shows the rear of the clubhead. Note the white mark, which acts as an aid to lining up the club with the ball.

RIGHT: A Centre-Shafted putter. Again, notice the nick on the top of the club face; the ball should be lined up with that mark when putting.

putter which suited him. But things only seemed to work for a while; whatever he tried, his nervous twitch invariably came back to haunt him. Nowadays he admits to owning 70 putters.

And if, like most of us, you consider that to be a large number, spare a thought for Arnold Palmer. He has 3,000 of them!

The great Palmer years were — let's say — 1958-64, a period when he was famous for his bold and highly effective putting. After that, his skills began to wane, and his putter collection grew, as he tried to retrieve the situation by buying putters galore, or trying clubs sent to him by admirers. Surprisingly, Palmer would have very little to do with new and innovative designs: most of his 3,000 are of the blade type with a rear flange. Palmer still likes to spend time in his workshop modifying some of his putters. He'll alter lofts, lies, weights and, by judicious use of a file, even shapes.

I don't suggest that this sort of activity will turn you into another Arnold Palmer, but such modification is worth considering. You may have noticed that your feel for weight can vary from day to day. If, for example, a putter begins to feel too light for you, then there's an easy remedy. Simply add some lead tape.

The type of putter favoured by many of the modern-day professionals. Note the yellow and red 'T' marker. This helps to line the ball up correctly at address.

It's surprising how few club players make use of this invaluable commodity, but take a look in a professional's bag and you'll find a very different story. Some pro's actually stick lead tape to *every* club, believing that they can 'fine tune' each to their own requirements by so doing. That may be going a bit far for most of us.

I wouldn't advise filing a putter, if only because the resale value might be reduced to nil. Club pro's will help you by altering the lie of a club, however, ensuring that it sits on the ground in mid-sole. Remember, also that you shouldn't have to move near to or further away from the ball because heel or toe is catching the turf.

Loft can also be altered, although the type of metal used may prevent this; manganese bronze, for example, has to be worked at very high temperatures.

All very interesting, but if you can find a club which suits you without alteration, then stick to it.

A basic Blade Putter with no marker on the top of the club face. This may be worth considering when buying a putter.

This Blade Putter clearly shows that modern-day putters do not have 'dimples' or grooves, unlike the hickory-shafted putter of yesteryear.

Putters past and present. While all different, the one thing they have in common is the face of club being at right angles to the floor.

A blade putter with hickory shaft and a very large-headed putter which became popular after Jack Nicklaus used one whilst winning the 1986 US Masters.

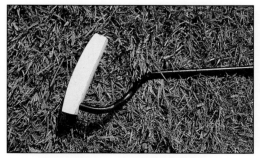

A Basakwerd putter. One of the oddest designs – yes, the toe does point towards your own toes when you use one.

CHOOSING A BALL

Golfers tend to be obsessed by length. Most will buy a ball which they think will carry and run the furthest. In contrast, the average tournament pro can hit it quite far enough for all practical purposes, enabling them to use an iron from the tee, and still reach the green on shorter par 5's with another iron club. They don't, therefore, choose for length, but rather for the amount of control a ball will give them. (Having said that, it's worth remembering that a good many of them are under contract to play a particular brand of ball, and receive bonuses for winning with it.)

Control arises from the ability to impart spin, A balata-covered ball will take much more spin than a solid one, providing more backspin and making it easier to draw or fade the ball. Some prefer a solid ball, however, relishing the definite feel it gives to the clubface. I remember Henry Cotton once remarking to me that he would have loved to have had the modern hard ball to putt with.

Cotton felt it would have helped him with problems on the greens, so the choice is worth thinking about. Do you prefer the feel of a harder or softer ball when putting? It could make all the difference.

Golf ball cleaners are inexpensive to buy and it is worth carrying one in your golf bag. Make sure your ball is clean before you putt. You can only lift the ball off the putting surface to clean it.

Golf balls come in varying colours. The traditional white ball remains the most popular and is the one that is used in competitive golf. When there is snow around a coloured ball is recommended.

CARE OF THE PUTTER

Most putters are made of reasonably hard metal, some very hard indeed. Such heads need very little protection, so not a few golfers use head covers to keep the club in a new condition.

Very little maintenance is needed because the putting stroke itself is hardly likely to do the club any injury.

Occasional attention to the grip is advisable. The putter is used more than any other club, so there is friction to smooth the surface and a gradual accumulation of grease and dirt.

Besides the condition of the putter grip, you might also consider a change. A great variety of shapes are available and it could be – at the simplest level – that a change from round to square, or vice versa, might be helpful.

Even if you can't see it, greens usually slope towards lower ground.

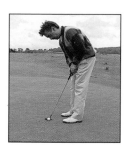

GETTING DOWN TO IT

Now – you've chosen your putter, and you have sorted out your grip. All you have to do now, is get out on the green and start getting the ball into the hole. Let's start with . . .

An exposed green will often putt faster than others because the wind dries it out quickly.

GRIP PRESSURE

Seve Ballesteros maintains that you should only hold a club firmly enough to stop it falling out of your hands. And that's for a *full* shot, where the clubhead may be moving at well over 100 miles per hour.

It follows, therefore, even allowing for Seve's genius, that there is absolutely no excuse for clinging on grimly, knuckles whitened, when you're indulging in the gentle art of putting. After all, you really only apply much force when you're using your putter as a 'Texas wedge', choosing to putt from well short of the green.

For some players, there can be an exception to the rule. When taking a short putt – say four feet or less – firming up the grip can help a more decisive stroke, and prevent the blade from wavering, becoming just a little more open or closed.

Trying to find the sweet spot.

An open, wide stance of around 1900.

For most of us, most of the time, however, touch is the name of the game. When muscles of fore and upper arm tighten – feel vanishes.

EXACT STRIKING

You know that glorious feeling. The one when the ball flies off an iron or wood, as sweetly as a bird. No jarring in the fingertips at all, and a stark contrast to the sensation one gets when hitting a full 1-iron on the bottom of the blade on an icy morning!

Obviously, you've found the sweet spot on the clubface. Everyone searches for that sensation on full shots, but how many of us even consider the matter when putting?

But – knowing where that 'sweet spot' is on your putter, and bringing it into contact with the ball, can save you shot after shot on the green.

 **ABOVE LEFT AND RIGHT:** Toes parallel to the target line.

Let's suppose you are facing a ten-yard putt, and have judged the pace and borrows of the green to perfection, and that your clubhead moves at exactly the pace you've decided upon. Then your ball will drop neatly into the hole. Obviously. I'm afraid not. Unless the strike from the sweet spot is perfect, you'll finish feet short.

So first you have to find out where that sweet spot actually *is*. Fortunately, that's not too difficult. Take a ball, preferably a hard one, and bounce it a good few times on your putter face. Because you're doing this randomly, you'll notice a fair amount of vibration along your putter handle. When you don't – you've found the sweet spot.

Having done that, you can then bounce the ball more carefully, until you've located the spot precisely. You can then mark it temporarily, remembering to make your mark more permanent, perhaps by making a nick at the top of the blade, a little later.

The obvious assumption is that you should be hitting any shot from what looks like the middle of the clubface, but this is often not so, and you'll probably need a little practice to adjust to the new position.

The putter on the left is standard length. That on the right encourages an upright stance for a tall golfer.

THE STANCE

Many great putters have adopted a very open stance, while others have stood in a closed position. They will all have

ABOVE: A jab putt, no follow-through.

RIGHT: This green is far from perfect. Assess the green's 'feel' when you first walk on to it and decide whether it is going to make your putt faster or slower. Don't forget, you are not allowed practice putts on the green.

made their choice after a great deal of experimentation. For most of us, however, a square stance will work best. This means that both toe tips will be parallel to the target line, between the ball and the point you're aiming at – which isn't necessarily the hole, when allowing for borrow.

Your distance from the ball will depend on a variety of factors, including length of putter shaft, your height, and whether you hold your hands high or low.

The ball itself may lie anywhere between the middle of the feet to a little ahead of the left foot – two extremes which have been used by a few successful players. Most players find a position somewhere opposite the left heel works best.

ANGLE OF ATTACK

The direction the putter head is travelling in when it strikes the ball is obviously important, but the angle of its path is equally so. There are only three possibilities – level, descending and rising. Great putters have used all three very successfully, but there are advantages and disadvantages with all three.

Take Gary Player. In spite of the fact that most players think they ought to get down in two from a reasonable position in a green-side bunker, the great South African will probably go down in history as the finest bunker player ever. He was, and is, superb from the sand, but the sheer quality of his short putting makes him look even better. After all, you can't get down in two if you miss the putt!

Player is one of the very few great putters whose clubhead is descending when it meets the ball. His short follow through makes the shot look like a jab.

ABOVE AND RIGHT: Sometimes you have to putt from an unusual stance. Grip down the shaft if you get in this position.

For most putters, the major advantage of the descending angle of attack is that a momentary backspin is imparted which takes some speed off the ball and enables it to be struck more definitely. This, however, becomes a disadvantage as putts get longer. Once feel for distance becomes involved, that jabbing action can't work for many people.

In 1987, Nick Faldo came in from the cold and won the Open at Muirfield. Over the next few years, as he added two US Masters titles, came within a whisker of the 1990 US Open, and won the 1990 British Open, we heard a great deal about his new swing developed with coach, David Leadbetter.

Faldo had always had a good long game, but inside himself, hadn't really believed that it was consistent enough when under extreme pressure. Faldo's 'new' swing is now part of legend, but his putting is equally remarkable.

There isn't much drama in watching a man hole out from four feet. It's exactly what everyone, from tournament professional to modest club player, is expected to do. The point is, that most *don't*.

Except Nick Faldo. He must, obviously, miss sometimes, especially from those fast downhillers with a drift to one side, but those apart. Faldo is, and has long been, arguably the best short putter the world has seen.

From whatever distance, Faldo's ideas about striking are the same, and diametrically opposed to those of Gary Player. His putting swing paths involve a low away swing, and meeting the ball at the equator, with the clubhead travelling upwards. He believes that this imparts topspin, and helps to get the ball rolling, rather than hopping, along quickly. This means a more gentle approach than the Player method, and gives Faldo the feel of stroking all his putts.

Nick Faldo often practises putting with a wedge, making sure that the upwards angle is maintained. If he swings through too low, he will produce a chip shot, making the ball leave the ground for a foot or two. If he makes contact in the middle, with the leading edge of the club travelling upwards, the ball will hug the ground, just as it does when using a putter.

Both of these methods work, for Player and Faldo and many others. Equally, great numbers of golfers have believed that there is no substitute for making the club follow low through the ball and on along the target line.

This is certainly an easier route to consistency. The other

When putting to the upper tier of a green, concentrate on distance rather than accuracy. If you don't strike the ball firmly enough, it may well end up back at your feet!

The Nicklaus position of the right elbow.

Putter grounded.

Putting with the sole off the ground.

two methods involve trying to deliver a glancing blow, imparting backspin or topspin, while keeping the clubhead low to the ground before and after impact with the ball does not. The only answer is to experiment to see which method suits you best.

HOW LOW?

Most of this is entirely obvious. The clubhead mustn't brush the grass because the merest suggestion of a bump, and the club, brushing against the grain of the green, will be checked more severely than you might think.

However, many players start from a position with the club resting on the ground. You can't really swing back from that position, because the first movement has to be to lift the club from the ground before swinging back, or to move back with a swing which is partly lift.

HEAD AND EYE

It's ideal to have the feeling that you are looking from behind the ball, along the target line. This is very much the position which Jack Nicklaus adopts, and his confidence in his method has enabled him to last for well over 30 years in competitive golf. In his great years, he very seldom had miracle days on the greens, but he always seemed to have the knack of holing the ones which really mattered.

Many golfers, however, won't find themselves happy with the Nicklaus position. It seems more natural to have the head over the ball, but – remember – don't just look at the top of it. That will slightly, but perhaps fatally, affect your feel for the stroke. After all, you are going to have to hit the *back* of the ball, not the *top* of it.

When preparing to make your putt, you will, inevitably, be taking one or two glances along the line. Taking too many is valueless, however; it just delays the 'moment of truth' when you have to hit the ball.

Looking along the line.

EVERY PUTT IS STRAIGHT

All TV watchers will have sometimes been amazed at the vast swing of the ball seen on the fast greens of the US Masters and Open. Even the much slower British greens can sometimes give a freakishly big swing, as when putting over some of the humps at St Andrews. Even so, the player should always think of these as straight putts: the ball is hit straight, the green provides the ball's lateral movement.

Low follow-through.

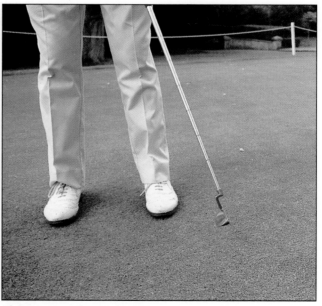

Club more on the rise here.

Plum bobbing standing behind the line.

Plum bobbing crouching behind the line.

LEFT: The two levels on this green add to difficulties of putting.

LEFT TO RIGHT, TOP TO BOTTOM: Medium-length putt with slight borrow from the left. This one fell short.

Nevertheless, your thinking has to change on any green with borrow. Let's take the short ones first – from, say, two feet to five feet.

The best method is to visualize the curve your ball will need to take, and the ideal pace for it to travel. The ball is then started on its way straight, aimed at a point along that curving path.

You can, however, take a very different attitude to the curving short putt, simply straightening the curve.

A ball borrows more when it is travelling very slowly. We've all seen that trickling ball move sharply sideways across the front of the hole, just when it seemed to be about to topple in at its last gasp. A brave putter simplifies things by hitting the ball more crisply.

Rather than aim at, perhaps, four inches from the hole when putting delicately, they know there will be little turn on a firm putt from close range. They might be able to aim just inside a lip.

Of course, there are perils. It's fatally easy, on a downhill putt on a fast green, for you to finish up further from the hole than you when you started – if you miss. So don't.

Unless confidence is high, however, most players discard this approach for a fast downhill putt. It's probably better to dribble the ball at the hole, in the knowledge that,

The high spots on greens dry out in hot weather (brown areas). Your ball will run more freely over these parts.

if you miss, you'll only be two or three feet beyond the hole, at worst.

For a medium-length putt (10–15 feet) your strategy needn't change much. However, even when putting firmly, you'll see that any borrow will start to take effect. You'll certainly be aiming outside the hole, but being firm still has the same advantages; a dying ball is a dying ball, and it will borrow just as much, however far it has travelled. A firm putt still makes the putt straighter.

Long putts present different problems of course. The thought processes are different when we say that every putt is straight. In this case you need to visualize the curving line of your ball, but it will still travel in a relatively straight line when it is travelling quickly. Try to hit straight along your chosen line, aiming at something – perhaps a lighter or darker blade of grass – and feel the pace that your ball should be travelling when it arrives there.

MOVING PARTS

I t has long been a truism of design that a well-engineered mechanism should have as few moving parts as possible. The same applies to the golf swing and, it follows, to the mini-swing that is the putting stroke.

As far as putting is concerned, the great golfers of the distant past were very wristy. They often saw putting as a matter of hinging the wrists to and fro, only allowing the arms to come into it for very long putts. Such ideas have long been discarded, and even reversed. Nowadays, the wrists only break when the distance to the hole is very great.

For at least a generation, from the end of World War I until the 1930s, Bobby Jones and Walter Hagen were the

Although this isn't a true two-tier green, this player would have found putting from further down the upslope difficult to judge.

models, simply because their stature as the two greatest golfers in the world was unassailable. They remained just as influential after they had disappeared from the scene, because no one in their class appeared for about ten years. Even when Henry Cotton, in Britain, and Sam Snead, Byron Nelson and Ben Hogan, in the United States, arrived, in the years either side of World War II, nothing much changed.

This was because Jones and Hagen were supreme putters and their successors didn't seem to be. Cotton never looked comfortable on the greens. Although he was competent, his success was invariably attributed to the rest of his game.

In the United States things were much the same. From 1944, Nelson produced an unerring straightness which no one has been able to match since, and which was probably paralleled only by Harry Vardon in his great years from 1896 to 1900. He didn't miss short ones, and didn't three-putt very often, but people saw him as a great golfer, not a great putter.

When Ben Hogan reached his peak from 1946 to 1953 or so, it was his long game people noticed. A few observers thought he was deadly from about eight feet or so, but that was it. He was very like Henry Cotton, in that both made full shots look easy, but neither was much imitated for their putting abilities.

Much the same can be said for Samuel Jackson Snead. He had the most oily and powerful swing ever seen, and his short game was every bit as good – apart from his short putting. Snead was superb on the greens from long range, but, so they say, was always likely to twitch from close to the hole. You couldn't emulate his long game, and his putting failings were to be avoided.

It took Bob Charles to change ideas about putting. Bob wasn't a bad golfer at all, even though he was left-handed, which always looks awkward and 'different'. His game was long enough – as opposed to 'long' – off the tee, and people, including his fellow professionals, considered him to be just an average golfer. So why was he so successful?

The answer, surely, lay in his putting. People who failed to take note of his consistency on the fairway sat up and took notice when the New Zealander reached the green.

Bob Charles really did have a new putting secret. He took the wrists out of the putting stroke. He imagined that his mini-swing came from his neck; from a joint just above the shoulders, and he *didn't break his wrists*.

Today, all the pro's believe the same, although they may have different ways of expressing the concept. Even when

Don't putt into bunkers! It's often been done here – the Road bunker at St Andrews.

49

The Ben Crenshaw arm position.

Keep that flow of the left elbow constant.

tapping it in from two inches, they use an arms-only movement and *don't break the wrists*.

Oddly enough, the most effective golfer of all time has been much less imitated. For many years, Jack Nicklaus was regarded as no more than an overweight, crew-cut kid who could lash the ball huge distances, and then muddle through everywhere else. In fact, Jack, himself, now sees his golf game that way through the '60s and into the following decade.

While he may not have been the longest hitter in the world, there weren't many who were longer, and most of *them* couldn't play the game at all the rest of the way. But it was years before many people realised just how good Nicklaus was on the greens.

Jack's great strengths were the ability to hit a vast distance, and then follow up with superb long irons, and mid-irons that were just about as good. After that, he showed no more than average pro talent – until it came to putting.

The Nicklaus method is still like no one else's. Mechanically, he seems to stand behind the ball, thrusting towards the hole with a right-hand-dominated stroke. Even so, it isn't a matter of hand action; rather a piston movement, from the shoulders with the left arm unbending, and the right side providing the momentum.

Ben Crenshaw emerged early in the 1970s and, although his game was different, was hailed as the new Nicklaus. It hasn't quite worked out for him, largely because of a tendency to hit wild long shots. As a consequence, he has earned a reputation as the best player of recovery shots on the US Tour. Fellow professionals think equally highly of his putting.

Unlike Jack Nicklaus, Crenshaw has seen his putting stroke widely imitated. He stands further away from the ball than most, and is different from Bob Charles in that his stroke looks arms-only. His method has enabled him to be a winner into the 1990s and has brought him one US Masters.

Like many professional, Ben Crenshaw has a collection of putters. Being a student of the history of the game, however, most of them are antiques. While playing, he has remained faithful to an early love; a Wilson 8802, which is a blade putter with a rear flange. As I've said before, if you find a putter you are happy with – stick to it.

But Ben could probably putt well with just about anything. During his Ryder Cup singles battle with Eamonn Darcy at Muirfield in 1987, he broke his putter shaft after just a few holes. A complete disaster, you may think, but although he eventually lost, it was his long game which let him down. He seemed to putt just as well with an iron.

Among top-class players, Crenshaw may well be the best putter of recent times, but Tom Watson commands a much higher profile on the greens. This stems from his record as the dominant force on the US Tour for several years and the holder of the best record in major championships over that period. With five British Opens, one US Open and two US Masters under his belt, he easily qualifies for a place high up in the all-time rankings.

It is said that, early in his career, Watson had a passion to play perfect golf: to hit all the fairways and greens in regulation strokes. In the end, the real world caught up with him, and realising that this was impossible, he proceeded to work, just as single-mindedly, on his short game. How well he succeeded is revealed by a body of opinion once held among his fellow professionals that, if all the players missed all the greens, then Tom Watson would be the only possible winner. Quite simply, the best, from close to the greens or on them.

Television cameras, with their concentration on putting, put Tom's skills under a ruthless spotlight. He is unusual in that his grip on the putter is firmer than most, an exception which doesn't disprove the general rule. Mentally a reincarnation of the young Arnold Palmer, he really believed that he could make every putt, realising that a sure way to fail in that is to fall short of the hole. Tom always 'gave the hole a chance', having confidence that he could hole those return putts from, let's say, five feet or so. Alas, he's far more tentative today.

That's one feature of his game which teaches a valuable lesson. Another is his belief that a constant angle of the left elbow is vital – another moving part which can be eliminated, just like the necessity to avoid breaking the wrists.

The short but challenging, 7th hole at Pebble Beach, California.

While many links courses are often relatively flat, their greens can be deceptively undulating.

You can analyse that by trying out a putting stroke for yourself. Experiment by allowing your elbow to change position, and also by maintaining the same angle. It won't be difficult to sense the very different qualities of strike you obtain if you let the elbow flex, as you try meeting the ball with the clubhead descending sometimes, and on the rise at others. Actually, the effect is much the same as if you have allowed the wrists to flex.

Tom Watson once gave a memorable demonstration of this during a television programme. With all the aplomb in the world, he rattled in a series of medium-length putts while retaining a constant left elbow, and then showed how inconsistent results became when he allowed it to flex. What was really memorable was the way he knocked in that sequence with total ease and nonchalance. Most of us would be happy to have holed just one of them!

It isn't as difficult as you may think to keep that elbow angle constant. All you need do is feel that your back-and-through movement is coming from the joint of the arms with the shoulders. It doesn't matter much what that elbow angle is, whether you start with your elbow fairly straight as Ben Crenshaw does, or bent as in the Tom Watson method. What does matter is that the amount of bend remains constant throughout your putting stroke.

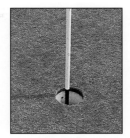

PUTTING – THE SHORT AND THE LONG OF IT

It's often been said that putting is a 'game within a game'. The idea is that wholly different skills are necessary on the green than are needed for the long game; that a star golfer must be able to propel the ball for 300 yards using a swing that travels at over 100 mph, but must also consistently get the ball into the hole from three feet.

I would go further. For me, short putting is a very different game from long putting. Once you are close to the

You must hole the short ones.

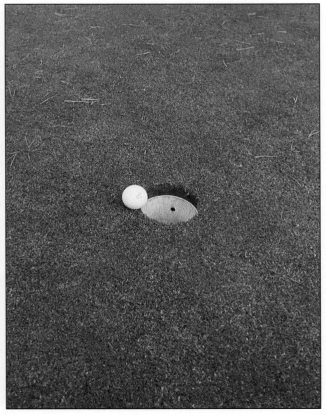

Toppling in from the side.

Don't try knocking them in one-handed.

Or reaching over the hole for a tap-in – this can happen and often does.

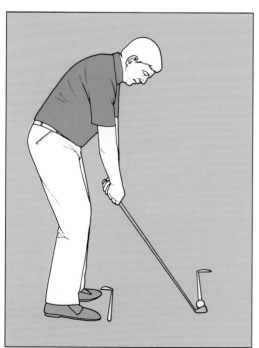

Using clubs to check body alignment to target line.

hole, there is relatively little need for feel, and the problem is fundamentally a simple one. All you need do is find a method which consistently moves the ball along your chosen line, into the hole, looming there, almost under your nose.

Sounds simple doesn't it? A child could do it, and many can – when it doesn't matter.

Some golfers don't need to change the mechanical method that experience has provided for them, when they reach the green. Others do. To recap some of the ground we've covered before, it may help to grip the club more firmly, giving you the feeling that you are striking more definitely, and also helping you to avoid the blade of your putter meeting the ball when open or closed.

That blade must be square with your target line. If you are not allowing for any borrow, imagine your putter head is sitting on one of a pair of parallel lines, the other running across the middle of the hole.

Don't just aim at the hole – that's much too vague. Pick a spot on the front or rear lip, according to taste, and aim at that. Presenting yourself with a tiny target forces you to be more precise.

ABOVE LEFT AND RIGHT: Plumb-bobbing. Hold your putter shaft vertically. If there's a side-slope between you and the hole, the theory is that the slope will show up as an angle of more or less than 90 degrees.

You do need to feel the strength of your stroke, even though, on a flat putt, there is little chance of your finishing disastrously far past the hole. Many short putts are missed when the player simply 'forgets' to hit the ball hard enough. He's thinking solely of direction, and finds it all too easy to come up six inches short on a 12-inch putt.

There is another point worth remembering, too. You'll recall that, in an earlier chapter, I have stressed the advantages of 'straightening out' curving short putts by hitting firmly. This doesn't apply significantly on flat putts, although a minute spike mark, or even the lie of the grass, may divert a slowly moving ball. That consideration apart, make your own decision about whether you feel happier when striking your putts crisply. If you decide you are, then you'll find yourself better served by striking firmly at the back of the hole.

Remember, also, that you need only be slightly off line for your ball to spin away from the edge of the hole. However, this isn't the case if your ball is moving very slowly. Here, you have three chances of the putt dropping: over the front lip, or from either side. And they can occasionally drop in from the back as well.

It's fatally easy to be careless with very short putts. Ask Hale Irwin, who has reason to know. He won the 1990 US Open after a vast putt across the 72nd green got him into the play-off, and a straightforward eight-footer settled things for him on the 91st. Yet seven years earlier, he had failed to tie for the 1983 British Open through a moment of sheer carelessness. His ball lay right on the lip of the hole, and he leaned over to tap it in nonchalantly.

And then missed the ball altogether.

So – don't take an age over it, but no matter how short the putt, do settle yourself into your normal putting stance, and make your normal stroke. No putting on the walk. No careless pushes or pulls.

Feel is what long putting is all about. Feel for distance, feel for the pace of the green, feel in your putting stroke. Even your club pro can only really help you with your basic method. The rest is down to experience.

Tournament players take a great deal of time pacing out their putts, examining the line from behind the ball and from either side. But I take leave to wonder if it really does them any good. I suspect that, most of the time, they are only confirming the impressions they got when they first walked on to the green.

Having said that, some things really are worth taking a look at, especially near the hole, when your ball will be travelling slowly and therefore most likely to deviate.

If the grain of the grass is against your putt, your chances of finishing short of the hole are increased. If the

LEFT AND RIGHT: Good feel for distance here. The ball is almost dead.

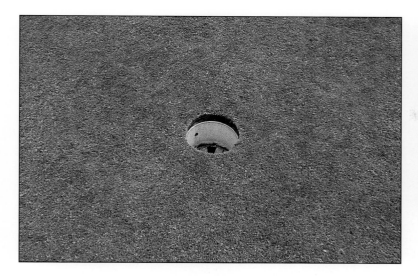

RIGHT TO LEFT, TOP TO BOTTOM: From a few feet away, closer still and finally, a look at how the hole is cut.

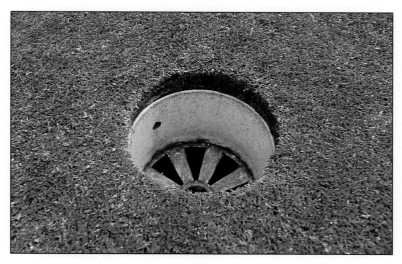

grain is away from you, you should be more concerned with making sure you're not likely to end up a long way past the hole. Around the hole itself, the grass is more likely to be flattened and worn. This may prevent your ball from stopping as quickly as a casual glance at the hole from a distance might have suggested.

A little experience will soon teach you about the effect of the putting surface on the distance your ball travels. You can hardly fail to notice, for example, that a close-cut surface has quite different characteristics from one showing a full day's growth.

Moisture, or lack of it, can also bring dramatic changes. Compare the behaviour of a burned-brown summer green with that of the same area during the thick, lush growing season. You'll also soon begin to notice the difference between an area of grass which has been shaded from the sun all day and one which has been in the sun all day.

These factors also need to be considered when there is a question of borrow rather than strength. Simply, there is more borrow when the surface is fast than when it is slow.

Looking at the hole.

These pine needles could deflect a putt, so move any debris on the line of your putt.

LEFT: When a green is close to a lake, it may putt slower on the side nearest the water.

Once you've made your judgements of pace and line, that information has to be translated to your putting stroke. In fact, line is of lesser importance unless there is severe borrow. On a 20-yard putt you are far more likely to be five yards long or short than you are to be five yards wide. Judgement of strength, and how to produce that exactly in your putting stroke, is therefore more vital than judgement of direction. That will largely take care of itself, assuming you have the basics right.

ABOVE AND RIGHT: How the grass has been cut affects the pace of a putt. When it's shiny you are with the cut, and pace will be quicker. It's a slower putt and against the grain when the grass looks darker. Putting across the line of cut makes little difference.

ABOVE: A parched summer green.

TOP AND ABOVE: After a day's growth, the grain produced by cutting has gone.

This is where the putter with a light grip comes into his or her own. No one can be successful in long putting unless the muscles of the arms remain relaxed, although some players would disagree as far as short putts are concerned.

Some golfers – Tom Watson, for example, who seems to give his putts a little punch with his lower arms – like to think that the very small amount of power needed is provided by the forearms. If you have a rather pendulum motion with the arms, however, try to feel the strength needed for the putt with the upper arm, muscles relaxed yet active.

Finding the sweet spot and exact striking are equally important. You can hit a short putt very poorly and still find the hole, but disaster is certain from long range. Tests using machines prove that, on a 60-foot putt, a ball struck one inch away from the sweet spot will finish 15 feet short of the hole. Reduce that error to a half-inch and you'll still be five feet short, with a three-putt looming.

It's more difficult to judge the line when shade and sunlight alternate on a green.

If part of a green has been in the shade, it will putt more slowly.

The same machine was used to compare strength and correct performance of actual strokes. Tournament professionals putted against it over 60 feet. The pro's holed just 3% of their shots. Even the 'perfect' machine only managed 20% – but invariably got the ball close to the hole.

The lessons are clear as regards long putting. A green isn't a snooker or pool table. It changes second by second, depending how each blade of grass is lying at the time. Holing out from a distance is, therefore, always something of a fluke.

Your approach for all those putts which lie between the obviously long, and the clearly short, should be the same as for long ones. From, say, 20 feet, tournament pro's still miss nine times out of ten (even the machine only managed 50%).

Once more, the lesson is that you should concentrate on getting the distance right and let nature take care of the line. Your target should be to get the ball close. *Feel* the distance and concentrate on a pure strike, rather than try to 'will' the ball along your imagined line into the hole.

TOP LEFT, RIGHT AND ABOVE: This putt is straight at the hole – but well short.

ABOVE: The putter can be your friend from unlikely positions – if you can develop feel for the run of the ball.

LEFT: Judging a slope like this takes extreme talent (St Andrews).

ABOVE AND RIGHT: Good feel for distance here.

SHORT OR LONG BACKSWING?

Here, you need to use your personal feel for the ball to arrive at an acceptable compromise. Backswing too short, and you'll find yourself forcing your putter head at the ball, because you haven't allowed yourself enough swing to produce the necessary amount of momentum. Too long and a whole new set of problems appear.

To start with, the more distance the club has to travel, the more chances there are of wavering or wandering off line. Mentally, you are also far more likely to feel doubts as your club moves back to the ball, a condition which often leads to your slowing the club down and hitting the ball less firmly than required.

In fact, there aren't really any firm rules to follow, although some pundits have tried to simplify things by

Huge slopes can be very difficult to judge (St Andrews).

An extremely difficult putt if your approach is past the hole.

stating how far back you should swing for a putt of – say –
30 feet as opposed to one of 20 feet. If you think about it, this
is absolute nonsense, because it makes no allowance for the
pace of the greens. That particular factor is a matter of
experience; of playing and practising on all varieties of
putting surface.

The only answer is to experiment until your backswing
is a matter that doesn't require thought, becomes automatic,
and works for you.

SHORT OR LONG FOLLOW-THROUGH?

The face of your putter is in contact with the ball for a tiny
fraction of a second, and this is true whether you jab at the
ball or putt with a smooth, flowing stroke and a relaxed
follow-through. So everything depends on what kind of action
gives you best results.

I have mentioned Gary Player as a great putter with a
'jabbing' action. It's always worked for him, and still does,
over a career of 30 years or more. Nevertheless, he once won
the US Masters after his wife suggested he revert to a
smoother stroke which had served him well at an earlier stage
in his development. He used it for a while, but eventually
returned to the tried and true method which he trusted more.

LEFT AND RIGHT: This is better. A confident
putter aims to be past the hole.

SPIN, MIND AND TWITCHES

In theory, jabbing down on the ball imparts backspin, and hitting it on the up results in topspin. Unfortunately, things aren't quite as simple as that.

Years ago, many golfers liked to use a putter with loft: greens weren't so smooth and consistent as today, and a degree of loft made the ball travel in the air for a short distance, so that the ball was well on its way before being checked or deflected for the first time.

With an elevated green, it can pay to putt your ball short, particularly when the ground is hard and dry.

Bobby Jones' famous putter, 'Calamity Jane', with which he achieved most of his successes, had a loft of some eight degrees, much the same as a rather straight-faced driver of today. 'Calamity', and her sisters, almost certainly gave some backspin, not an advantage in putting, although that early travel off the ground could be useful on poor winter greens.

During medium or long putts, the ball travels off the ground for a short distance (depending on the length of the shot), then skids for a while, before rolling for the rest of its journey.

It is even possible to apply cut or hook spin to a putt. Old-time players liked to cut the ball into a right-to-left slope, believing that this kept the ball on line, just as if they were hitting a wood or iron into a right-to-left wind. However, the spin only lasts for a very short time, for that period when the ball is travelling in the air, or skidding. After that, the ball's forward momentum rapidly removes any sidespin.

TOP LEFT AND RIGHT, AND ABOVE: Every putt is *hit* straight, even though this one *travelled* left to right.

The ball is skidding here. You can see from its shadow that the ball is off the putting surface.

The putter on the right is favoured by players who are struck down with the 'yips' – that inability to hit the ball. The extension of the putter is rested against the player's chin and held with one hand. The other hand does the work.

LEFT: Although the fairway is brown, there's nothing wrong with this putting surface.

ABOVE AND OPPOSITE: You must get the medium-length putts stone dead.

'YOU PUTT INSIDE YOUR MIND'

At the peak of Tony Jacklin's career, which covered the years 1968–73, his fellow professionals thought him nearly infallible in the vital three-to-four-foot range. For the rest, he was a 'streak' putter. There were days when he couldn't go wrong, and others when he came well down from the heights.

Those short putts are a matter of technique and confidence. If you *know* you're going to hit them straight from short range, then you'll hole the lot – and much the same is true when you are just a few feet further away, say, up to about eight feet.

Tony lost all certainty. He felt he had to hit his approach shots very close indeed to give him birdies. Similarly, he felt he had to get his long putts very close to avoid three-putting.

There were still the 'golden days' when the battle 'inside your mind' was won. Alas, they didn't come frequently enough to keep Tony Jacklin at the top of the tree.

The pressures of tournament golf are very great, and those of a major championship even greater. After all, a man is playing for his livelihood, wealth, even a kind of immortality, but the club golfer doesn't live in an entirely different world. It is often very important for them, too, to play well, to win matches and competitions.

The importance of an event is relative, and it is that importance which applies the pressure. Regarding it all as unimportant, even treating it casually, doesn't help. And there has to be a balance between producing as good a performance as possible, with maximum concentration, and collapsing under the strain.

It isn't easy. You have to divorce yourself from the occasion – say, going for a good score in a strokeplay competition – and think only of the putt you are facing.

The buzzing of the flies, your partner's infuriating habit of shuffling their feet, any extraneous distraction – they're all irrelevant. So are thoughts about what a disaster it will be if you fail to get this 12-footer stone dead, and miss the next one.

No. It isn't easy, but it has to be done. Concentrate on the job in hand, and ignore everything else.

LIVING WITH A TWITCH

Call it a 'twitch', 'the yips', 'jerks' or whatever: 'Once you've had 'em, you've got 'em.' That was the opinion of Henry Longhurst, the best golf writer of modern times.

If you haven't a clue what I'm talking about, then perhaps you shouldn't read any further. However, I've never heard of a case of this dreaded disease incurred by simply reading about it, so it's probably safe to continue.

The twitch is a muscular spasm of hands or arms which can occur during the putting stroke. At best, it means a poor ball strike: at worst, your putter can propel the ball clean off the green.

Many great players have suffered, and many have been forced out of competitive golf. In fact, more have left the game this way than through the sheer decline of physical powers in the long game.

I remember talking to ABC and BBC golf commentator Peter Alliss about the dreaded scourge. Peter was a top British star in the 1950s and 60s, and although still an automatic choice for Ryder Cup teams, retired from tournament play in 1969.

'You know,' he said, 'I can even be putting casually at a chair leg, but if I say to myself, "this is for real", I'm likely to twitch it.'

Bernhard Langer provides a much better-known example. Twitching usually seems to arise after years of tournament play, but Bernhard's case wasn't like that. He twitched as a teenager, and has had to endure severe attacks ever since. If anyone should know a cure, he should.

Like all other sufferers, Langer never has found a permanent remedy, but he has learned to live with it well enough to win a Masters, and a host of other titles throughout the world.

Bernhard's twitch seems to occur in the left wrist. He has learned to live with it in three distinct phases, and in three different ways. Early in the 80s he found a putter which he really liked, the twitch disappeared, and almost overnight he became one of the best putters on the European Tour. Sam Snead had the same experience in the 1940s.

For Langer, the magic putter failed after a couple of years or so. His next solution was to play short putts with left hand below right, reverting to his normal reverse overlap for the longer ones. It's highly unusual to change grips in this way, and many people wondered how he decided which grip to use. Did he change over at a certain distance from the hole? Not a bit of it. The normally methodical German was more instinctive than that. He just changed over 'when it felt right'.

In 1988 that cure failed too, to such an extent that he took five putts on one green during the 1988 Open. After long experimentation, he arrived at a truly strange grip. The left

LEFT: A putting green will nearly always slope towards water, even if very slightly.

hand remained below the right, but he now held his left forearm with the fingers of his right hand, while the palm helped support the putter. In effect, if a nervous spasm was causing his left wrist to twitch, then his new grip made the club shaft into a splint. Bernhard Langer was on his way once more.

I'm not suggesting that Langer's splint technique is an answer to problems for the golfer at club level, but if you are afflicted, then there are advantages to making changes, even quite minor ones.

Identify, as closely as possible, where that tremor is. Then change your stroke so as to take that troublesome area out of it.

Many club golfers don't realise that they have a tremor. It occurs only occasionally, for example, when faced with an important putt, downhill with a left-to-right break. The shorter the putt, the worse the twitch, because the shorter the shot, the more shame-making it is to miss.

If such a golfer misses, they put the blame on lack of concentration, misjudgement of line, looking up too quickly and any other reason they can think of. But it's really all an excuse. Anything to avoid the admission that they have that fatal, nervous spasm.

The practice green, obviously feeling the effect of a hot dry summer. In such conditions the greens play faster than normal.

PUTTING FROM OFF THE GREEN

Remember that the putter isn't restricted to the putting surface. Let's look at an extreme example.

Once upon a time, two good young players arrived at the tee of a par 3 in a friendly practice round. One, the club champion incidentally, hit a 6-iron to about 10 feet and stood aside. His playing companion then started to debate about which club he should use. Was it a hard 6-iron for him, or perhaps a more relaxed 5-iron? Or, because the ground was

If your ball lands on the wrong half of a double green, you could be faced with a very long putt.

firm, perhaps he ought to pitch well short of the green and let the ball run on? That might be an 8-iron shot.

'Look,' said the club champion, 'if you're a real golfer, you ought to be able to play this 160-yard hole with just about any club in the bag. Play a running punch shot with a 4-iron, hit a high fade with a wood, hood a wedge. You can even play it with a putter.'

With these final words, he snatched his blade putter out of his bag and, without a glance towards the green, swung.

Cleanly struck, the ball flew off on line for the gap between two bunkers guarding the front left and right of the green. With its low trajectory, it pitched well short of the green but held its line and ran towards the flag. And on. And on. And in.

A hole in one is as good a way as any to prove one's point. His companion has, however, been trying to get his own hole in one with a putter from time to time ever since. Without success.

So I'm not suggesting that a putter is often going to be the best club selection for a shot of 160 yards.

But it can come into play far more often than you might think. We are too inclined to think of golf as a game played by the air route. We dream of shots that soar upwards and plummet down at the flag, bounce once and come to a stop, stone dead by the holeside. There seems to be less glory – some think it's almost cheating – to bumble the ball along the ground. So here are some situations when the putter can give you a good result when it's not the conventional choice of club.

FROM THE FRINGE

I must admit that quite a few golfers do believe that putting from the fringe of the green is socially and morally acceptable, even if chipping is 'the proper golf shot'. Unless you are a very good chipper of the ball, the chances are you'll get a better average result using your putter. Put it to the test in practice and notice these things in particular. From say 10 yards or so, you'll probably feel reasonably satisfied if you chip to 2 yards. Yet when you get exactly that result with your putter, you'll probably feel you've made a bad putt. If those are your feelings, the messages are obvious. For you, the putter is an easier club to use in this situation. So use it.

RIGHT: A well-protected two-tier green.

Ian Woosnam about to take on a tricky putt.

FROM A GREENSIDE BUNKER

To putt successfully from a bunker, three factors must be in your favour.

(1)   There must be no front lip at all on the bunker to stop or divert your ball.

(2)   The sand must be firm rather than soft and fluffy. If it's soft, your ball won't roll freely over the surface but will stop quickly. The ideal time to use a putter is when the sand is wet after rain or as a result of the greens being watered.

(3)   You must have a clean lie – that is, the ball must be entirely, or almost entirely, above the sand. Once it is down just a little, you may succeed in moving the ball out of the bunker but judgement of how firmly to strike is impossible.

IN A BIG WIND

The higher your golf ball flies, the more it is affected by the wind. This, of course, applies just as much when you're near the green as for long shots. The way to keep it as low as possible is by using your putter. Whether the wind is behind you or in your face makes little difference.

It will still affect how far your ball runs, but far less so than if you play a high pitch. The difference is so great, in fact, that you need make little allowance for it at all.

THE TEXAS WEDGE

Texas is famous for producing golfers who know how to play in strong winds. If they don't learn, they might as well give up the game. This is true also of golfers who play on seaside links, high moors and heathlands. You seldom encounter a totally still day.

So what is this wedge? A putter. The nickname came about when other American golfers noticed how often Texans used their putters from well short of the green – from normal wedge distance in fact. This can be up to 120 yards but it would probably be foolhardy to use a putter from more than 50 yards from the green.

Texans and other golfers don't confine use of the putter from long range only to windy weather. They also use the club when they feel they are going to get a better result than when playing a pitch shot.

The key point to bear in mind is that the putter is simply the easiest club to use. The shaft is short, which means that your hands are nearer the ball than with any other club. That makes a golf stroke just that little bit easier. The lack of loft also makes a consistent result from a given impact speed much more attainable.

Many golfers never attempt to use the putter from long range. As I mentioned earlier, there is a strong feeling that 'it isn't golf' and that you look silly if you putt and finish either

TOP, ABOVE AND LEFT: Using a putter from off the green can produce more accurate results than those afforded by a lofted club.

many yards short of the green or way through the back. But this can happen with other clubs as well.

Experience is necessary. In the first place, you are hitting the ball much harder than normal. From being an always gentle stroke, the putt becomes quite firm. I don't think you can expect to get reasonable results if you try the shot every once in a while.

Practice, and on-course experience, will soon teach you a lot about how the ball runs, even over quite uneven ground. You can even putt over semi-rough, provided it isn't close-knitted.

Remember, earlier golfers must have consistently used their putters once they were near the greens. Why? Well, even though they did have lofted woods, pitching clubs as such didn't exist. So they putted instead. What irons they had were really intended for escaping trouble – bunkers, rough and ruts (no relief in far-off days!). Otherwise, a lofted wood, such as the baffy, was the club to pitch with and you wouldn't think of using it for anything under 80 yards.

The Texas wedge can be used over both wet and dry ground. Many prefer to use the shot only when the ground is dry and firm – when it's a little more like a putting green.

However, the shot can be equally, perhaps more, effective in the wet. The little bumps your ball strikes will be softer and divert your long putt less. The greens will also be considerably slower, which means less likelihood of a clumsy long putt racing through over a fast dry putting surface.

PUTTING OVER SEVERE UNDULATIONS

This time your ball is quite close to the green but with a bank between you and the hole, with the flag set close to that bank. This is the situation when you'll often hear a television commentator at a tournament say, 'He hasn't got much green to work with.' The commentator means that the golfer playing, for example, a short pitch shot, must be very precise. Their ball must only just clear the bank and reach the putting surface since the hole is only a very few yards onto the green.

In this case, the experienced golfer may think the putt is the percentage shot. As long as the grass is closely mown, it may well work better.

It all depends on how you see it and where your skills lie. Mark Calcavecchia, then British Open champion, was playing the Old Course at St Andrews in the Dunhill Cup in 1989.

LEFT: Of course, putting can be the least of your problems!

ABOVE AND RIGHT: You often get a better result when putting, rather than chipping, from the fringe of the green.

The Old Course has many double greens, with the result that a player can be on undulating surfaces, perhaps 50 yards further away from the hole than they are accustomed to.

Calcavecchia certainly wasn't used to it. He aroused quite a storm amongst both St Andreans and the press by wedging to the hole instead. Divots flew from the sacred turf. Calcavecchia repaired the damage on both occasions he tried the shot with exemplary care, but it still didn't satisfy onlookers.

Under the rules of golf he was fully entitled to wedge away on the greens to his heart's content, though I suspect many golfers wouldn't have known this. Mark later said that he just wasn't used to putting from such great distances and felt he had no chance of getting his ball close – but he was used to short wedge shots.

Ironically, both the Calcavecchia wedge shots were poor. He would almost certainly have done better with his putter. And that's the lesson of my story.

PRACTICE ROUTINES

The first thing to bear in mind is that your golf club practice green is probably nothing like the ones you'll encounter out on the course. It may not have been constructed in the same way, not cut to the same rhythm, and it isn't likely that any consistent attempt has been made to ensure that it plays at the same speed as the others.

This is a point you should certainly take into consideration, especially if you decide to take a few putts before an important round. It's preferable to limit your long-putt practice to getting the feel of your putting stroke, and making sure that your strike is in good order. There's little

Putting becomes a lot easier if you can put your approach shot onto the right tier of the green!

Many prefer to aim at the hole . . .

. . . but sometimes there's no need. Concentrate on your stroke and ball strike.

point in hitting a lot of putts to distant targets as if you were playing the actual course.

Short putting, on the other hand, won't do you much harm, because feel for pace is less important. The approach you use will depend on your own mental make-up. If missing a few very short ones is likely to damage your confidence, then try to be casual about the whole thing; concentrate on a good putting stroke and exact striking rather than trying to sink every putt. There's no real need even to aim at the hole.

On the other hand, it might suit your psychology best to pretend it's all for real. In that case, take care over every putt, telling yourself, 'It's this one for the championship.' Concentrate on short putts and maintain some method.

It can boost your confidence to hole a few from very short range, and then gradually move further away: if you miss one – start over.

But don't be content to keep putting along the same line. It's better to avoid that sort of sheer mechanical repetition by moving around the hole and *forcing* yourself to think about every putt.

And finally – don't spend too long on the green. Remember, you're going to be driving off from the first tee soon, and you don't want to cramp your style for that vital moment!

GENERAL PUTTING PRACTICE

Concentrate, first of all, on checking over your putting stroke, something which can be done at home, or even at work.

Set up close to a wall, playing parallel to it. If your putter head makes contact with the wall when you are making your stroke, then you have some valuable information.

If you hit it on your backswing – that's bad news. It tells you that you aren't taking your club straight back, let alone along the preferable slightly-inside trajectory. If that kind of take-away persists, then you're going to be cutting across the ball.

Alternatively, you can lay another club down, and proceed as before, using the shaft as an indication of basic faults in your stroke. When you are satisfied that your stroke mechanics are in working order, you can set it the task of actually sinking putts.

Practice putting from different directions.

The 18th at St Andrews.

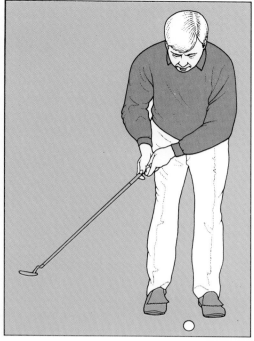

No wrist break in the putting stroke.

TOP AND ABOVE: Think about why you missed. Using just one ball can make each putt seem more important – especially if you don't like too much walking.

Don't indulge in long practice sessions, but make your practice intensive, and as real as you can. Avoid aimlessly and quickly striking a succession of putts, whether long or short. Tell yourself that each putt matters, and after each putt, pause to think out why you succeeded or failed that time.

It's a good idea not to use too many balls, and a better one to make your practice as competitive as possible. One way of doing this is to use two balls, imagining you have a match on – Curtis Strange against Nick Faldo, for example.

Better still, ask a real-life opponent to join in. Play for enough money to hurt, but not to wound – although Lee Trevino once said that real pressure is playing for $5 when you haven't got $5.

Who knows? You might become another George Low.

He was a US tournament player who found that he wasn't really good enough to make a living at it, even though he was outstanding on the greens. Accordingly, he took to hanging around the practice greens, playing all-comers for money.

It paid off a lot better than tournament golf.

RULES AND GOLF COURSE BEHAVIOUR

The first action a player should take is to repair their pitch mark. This is probably best done with the well-known fork-like tool. Acceptable substitutes include a tee peg or pocket knife. The aim is to lift out the indentation your ball has made. There will always be one, except when the greens are very hard or if you've played only a short shot in. If you cannot find your mark, repair one or more others instead. You'll then be a saint where so many other golfers are sinners. When you've lifted the turf, gently tamp it down flat with the sole of your putter. Don't use your feet; you'll merely replace one kind of damage with another – spike marks.

All this can, and should, be done quickly: golf can become agonizingly slow once players reach the putting surface. Let's treat this aspect of behaviour towards your fellow golfers first (the people waiting behind you).

Quickly decide who is furthest from the hole and is therefore first to putt. An exception would be if one of our imaginary fourball is in a bunker. He or she should play first, even though they may well be nearest the hole. The player may have to swing the club quite fast if they have a buried lie and a bad shot would mean the ball whizzes across the green. This change in the normal order of play is simply for safety reasons.

One of the non-putters should be stationed at the flagstick and either attend it or take it out, depending upon what they are asked to do. While this is done, they shouldn't either stand too close to the hole or on the line of any other player's putt; as this creates spike marks.

While anyone is putting, the other players should stand still, not either immediately behind or beyond the line of putt. This is to avoid distracting the putter. They should also be careful to make no noise. Also be careful not to cast a shadow on or near the line of putt.

Each player, when walking to the putting position, should have the line of putt of the other players in mind. Either walk around this line or take a stride over.

Players will often be asked to, or choose to, mark their balls on the green. The purposes are several: to avoid their being struck by another ball; to remove them as a distraction when there is only

an outside chance of their being struck; to clean them; to examine them for suspected damage and to set the ball down in a position the player finds useful. (Many like the writing to run horizontally across the equator of the ball; some might like the writing, still central, to run vertically; others might prefer to set the number exactly in the centre with the idea of bringing the sweet spot of the putter exactly into contact with this number.)

Much of this is a matter of personal taste. How you mark the ball isn't. This should be set down snugly behind the ball – not between ball and hole. Use a small coin or one of the variety of small discs with a spike.

Occasionally, your marker may be on, or near to, someone's putting line. You will then be asked to move your marker. There is a correct way of doing this. With the ball in place, measure a putterhead's distance away, pick up the ball, set it down against the toe of your putter and then re-mark the ball. Carry on in the same way if you are asked to move further.

All this shouldn't be allowed to take your ball either nearer or further away from the hole, so aim at some convenient point at right angles.

Alas, not a few golfers over the years have used marking their ball to provide opportunities to get it just a little nearer the hole. While there is no significant advantage in doing this on the tee (by playing from an inch or so in front of the tee markers), this can be very different on the green. Here, a couple of inches or so can have a great effect on the golfer's confidence. To him or her, an 18 inch putt may be the easiest thing to hole successfully. Doubts may seep in at 20 inches.

Professionals have been caught out cheating when marking their golf balls on the green and have been banned from the game.

Greens are the most delicate surfaces on the golf course. So far, by repairing pitch marks, we've done one job. If you are using a trolley or cart, this obviously should not be taken onto the putting surface, but you must also avoid the closely mown surrounds. At one time, golfers used to place their bags carefully on the greens, but this is frowned upon today. Instead, lay them down on the surrounds or rougher ground somewhere near your route to the next tee, to save time later on.

Try to avoid excessive marking of the putting surface with your feet. This can happen when a player, for example, twists about in mental agony when a putt narrowly misses. If you do transgress, repair the damage before you leave the green.

You can also cause damage with your putter, and that's aside from banging it on the turf in fury! Don't thrust it into the hole after putting with the aim of flicking the ball out. This can scar the edge of the hole. Don't lean heavily on your putter at any time and, when retrieving your ball from the hole, don't lean on it to help keep your balance. You shouldn't really need a prop for this simple act – though most professionals seem to!

When you arrive on the green, your preparations for putting should be made as quickly as your temperament allows. There's no excuse for any delay once you've completed play. Your clubs should be on your route to the next tee (not abandoned at the front of the green, where you remain in range as you collect your clubs and delay the following games). Get moving!

Though not so much as teeing grounds, putting greens are well defined, although by no means regular in shape. The rules that govern play on the greens are also simpler than for play on the rest of a golf course.

You can remove all loose impediments on the green. This also includes any under your ball where you simply mark, lift, remove the offending item and replace your ball. Beware, however, of being accused of testing the surface of the green. For instance, brushing the putting surface with your fingers or palm could well enable you to decide the grain of the grass and is not allowed. Avoid offending by sweeping away such impediments as leaves or pine needles with the back of your hand or putter and lift them individually if there are not too many.

Remember that you, your caddie or partner can help you decide where to aim your putt, but no one may make a mark and may only point, not lay a finger on the ground.

If you strike another ball, this means a penalty (different for stroke and match play) and striking the flag incurs a two-stroke penalty if you are on the putting surface rather than the fringe.

Remember there are also rules about how you stand to the ball. Years ago, golfers who developed a putting twitch found that a croquet stroke brought a cure. They acquired a mallet-like putter and stood astride the line, the ball between the legs. The club was held at the top with the left hand and the strike came from the right hand, well down the shaft. Sam Snead was a great player who found this method brought relief from his twitches on the greens. Perhaps unkindly, golf's authorities banned the method. Although it is unlikely to affect you, remember that leaning over the hole, when you've sent a short putt a very few inches past, usually means that you will have a foot on either side of the line – and have broken the rule.

'The Blackheath Golfer', a 1778 engraving by Lemuel Abbott. It is the earliest depiction of an English golfer, believed to be William Innes, captain of the Blackheath Club at the time.

GLOSSARY

Baffy: a lofted wood with a short shaft, once used for pitching to greens.

Balata: a soft golf ball covering which in theory provides more adhesion between ball and clubface. This leads to greater backspin, but the balls become scuffed more easily.

Blade putter: a putter more like an iron in design, because it too has a blade (and often a rear flange) rather than, for example, being more like a mallet or coke bottle shape.

Borrow: the slopes on a green which cause the ball to curve in the course of a putt.

Centre-shaft: a design of putter popular for many years. The essential feature is that the shaft is not fixed at the heel. Instead, it is fixed considerably nearer the centre, so that the sweet spot is only a little towards the toe of the club in relation to where the shaft is joined to the clubhead.

Cut: a form of spin applied to the ball. It causes a left-to-right spin and shape of shot.

Dying ball: a ball still moving but coming close to the end of its travel. In putting, many like to reach the hole with the ball moving very slowly indeed; others prefer a firmer strike to 'straighten' the borrow and are prepared to accept the possibility of a testing return putt when they miss.

Equator: an imaginary line running horizontally around the middle of a golf ball.

Fade: a shot which at first flies straight and then begins to curve left to right late on in flight.

Flange: a body of metal added to the sole or rear of a club. In the case of a putter, the main purpose is to provide more weight.

Flat putt: a putt without borrow.

Flex (of a shaft): bend.

Follow-through: that part of the golf swing which takes place after impact between club and ball. Often applied to the end of the swing alone.

Grain: the direction of growth of grass on a green. When the growth is away from the player and along the line of putt, the ball will travel further for the same strength of strike – and vice versa.

Grip: the action of holding a golf club.

Hickory: the type of wood most frequently used for golf club shafts until steel was introduced in the late 1920s. Its use today is mainly confined to a limited number of putters. Hickory clubs are more difficult to use, for most, because the shaft is twisted as well as bent. By comparison, steel shafts have little such torque (twist).

Hood: to strike the ball with the hands ahead of the clubhead at the time of ball strike. Depending on the variation of this hand position, the loft is either slightly or considerably reduced.

Hook: movement of the ball from right to left. The ball usually begins by travelling right of the target line and then begins curving left.

Jerks: the term has the same meaning as 'yips' and 'twitch'. All refer to an involuntary nervous movement, usually in the putting stroke but which can also occur in other short shots. This nervous movement is usually located in the hands, arms or wrists. Many great players have seen their careers come to an end as a result of this problem, frequently occurring on the greens and most often during very short putting.

Interlocking: a method of gripping where the little finger of the right hand and the forefinger of the left hand are entwined.

Lateral movement (on the greens): ball movements to either side.

Leading edge: the front rather than rear edge of an iron club or putter.

Loft: the slope on the face of a golf club.

Mini-swing: the golf swing in miniature.

Open stance: standing to the ball with left foot further away from the target line than the right.

Overlapping: grip of the club in which the little finger of the right hand rests on, or just beyond, the forefinger of the left hand.

Punch: manner of hitting a golf ball where the forearms dominate and there is less wrist movement than usual.

Recovery shots: these occur after a player has hit a shot into some difficulty. If the player can retrieve the situation completely they have 'recovered'. For example, if a player hits into a greenside bunker but putts their sand shot close to the hole, that is a recovery. If, however, they merely escape from that same bunker and not near to the hole, that is not a recovery.

Reverse overlap: a grip used in putting and sometimes for very short shots from quite close to the green. The player takes their left forefinger off the club and rests it in one of several possible positions over the fingers of the right hand. It is called 'reverse', because the left hand is involved in the overlapping, rather than the little finger of the right hand.

Royal and Ancient: the golf club in St Andrews, Scotland, much involved in administering aspects of the game of golf. One of its prime responsibilities is laying down the rules of golf in most countries.

This it does in conjunction with the United States Golf Association, which bears this responsibility in North America. The R and A, as it is often called in brief, also organizes the British Open Championship, and several other championships for amateurs. It also plays a role in the development of golf.

Schenectady: a mallet type putter with the shaft fixed towards the centre of the clubhead. It was designed early this century and became very popular after the American Walter Travis won the British Amateur using one in 1904. Centre shaft putters were banned by the R and A a few years later (but not the United States Golf Association) and the ban remained in force until 40 years ago. This was one of the main points which divided the two organizations as regards the rules of golf.

Sole: that part of a golf clubhead which rests on the ground when the ball is addressed.

Square stance: standing to the ball with both feet an equal distance from the target line.

Straight-faced: a club, usually said of a long iron, when there is little loft on the clubface.

Streak putter: a player who putts brilliantly but only in relatively short spells, perhaps a few holes, a round of golf or even a whole tournament. A player who is not recognized as being a consistently good putter.

Sweet spot: the small area on the putter face which gives the designed results when the ball is struck. The ball should then travel the anticipated distance. It will travel less far the further the strike is from the sweet spot.

Topspin: where the ball rotates in flight, or from the clubhead, with top of the ball moving towards the bottom in a forwards direction. Many consider this an impossibility in putting until the ball ceases to skid over the green and to begin rolling. However, a player can reduce the amount of backspin which naturally occurs by striking the centre of the ball on the upswing and by using a putter with very little loft.

Twitch: *see* 'jerks'.

Yips: *see* 'jerks'.

INDEX